For

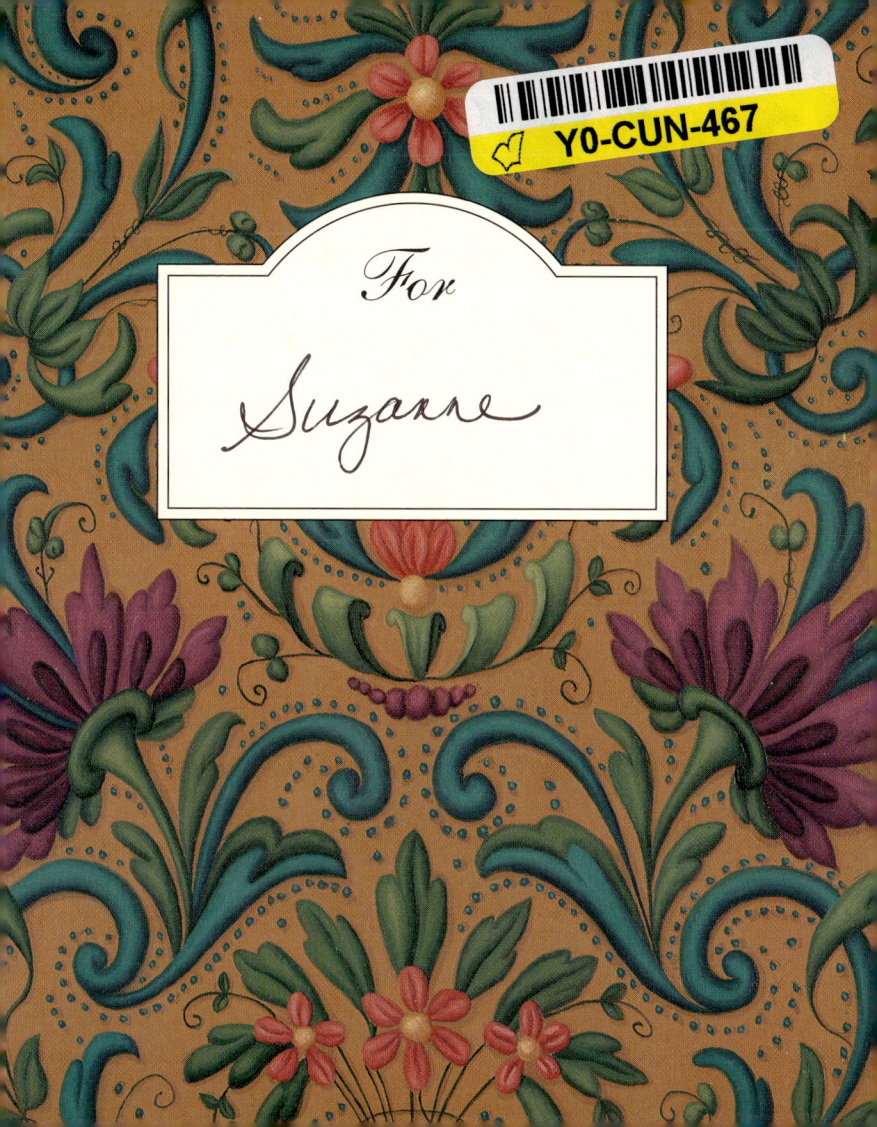

Suzanne

Suzanne,

This chapter in the journey of life is so precious!

Live every moment & enjoy everyday!

After this chapter, it will never be the same.

It only gets Better!

Good luck!

I love you

Lorri

THAT SPECIAL

Mother

From Pregnancy to Motherhood

Edited by Phyllis D'Aprile Alston

Designed by Michel Design

PETER PAUPER PRESS, INC.
WHITE PLAINS · NEW YORK

*For Rodney, Sr., Rodney, Jr., and Tiffanie Rose,
without whom I would not be
That Special Mother*

Copyright © 1994
Peter Pauper Press, Inc.
202 Mamaroneck Avenue
White Plains, NY 10601
All rights reserved
ISBN 0-88088-868-7
Printed in Singapore
7 6 5 4 3 2 1

Jacket background illustration by Grace De Vito

Introduction

*You were not yet conceived—and were
 already in my heart.
You were not yet born—and I was full
 of longing for you.
You were not yet a day old and we had
 a lifetime together.
You were my child, I was your mother—
 forever.*

NICOLE BEALE

Pregnancy lasts only nine months. This Keepsake will last forever. It will guide you from month to month through childbirth, and will serve as a cherished memento of your individual experience. The selection of quotes reflects a uniquely female perspective with humor, wisdom, and honesty. Also, blank pages are provided for you to record your feelings, thoughts, and observations. Most of all, *That Special Mother* offers a glimpse into this time in your life and into your baby's entry into the world. So turn the page, and embark on this exciting journey of life!

Month by Month

FIRST MONTH

Menstruation hasn't occurred. Otherwise, things are not very different for you. You are not aware of it, but the placenta has been developing.

By the end of the first month, the baby, which started as a cluster of cells, is ¼ inch long and looks a little like a tadpole.

Doctors often recommend taking vitamins and folic acid, both of which are important for the development of the fetal spine. Cramping is common at this stage.

In order to determine your baby's due date, see chart on page 54.

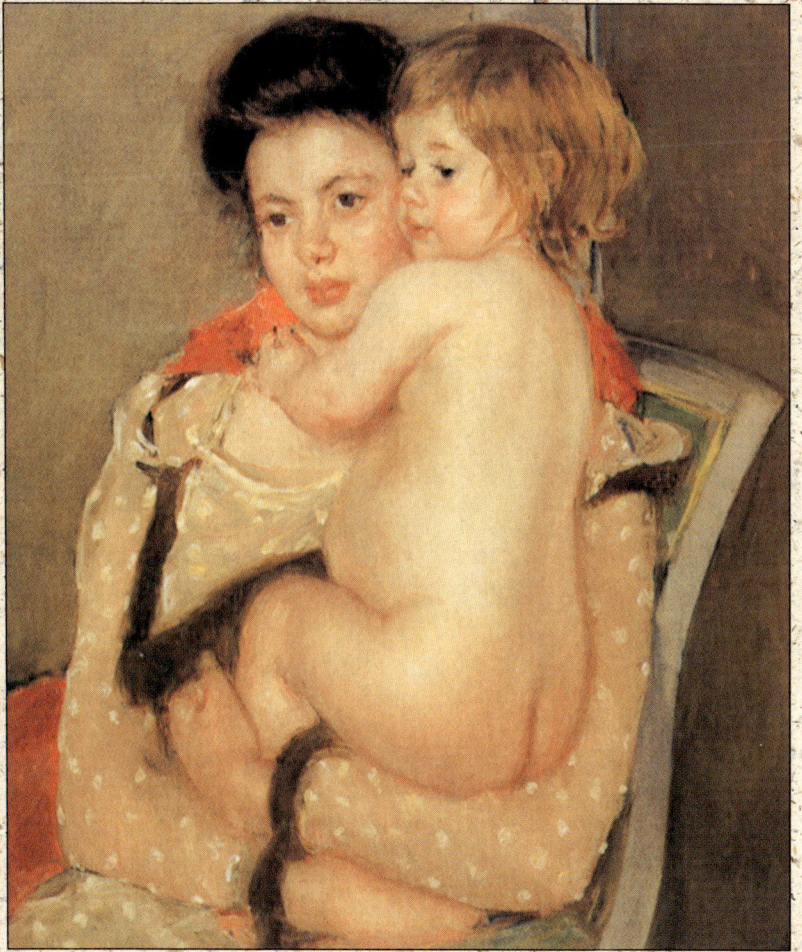

We're more thrilled than we ever imagined! Somehow I never actually thought this would happen to me. It may sound funny, but I'm so happy with myself. It's as if I am the first person ever to be pregnant! I can't think of an act that's more creative or more fulfilling.

ANONYMOUS

How can one accept crazy creatures who deem it a misfortune to get pregnant and a disaster to give birth to children? When it's the greatest privilege we women have compared with men!

GOLDA MEIR

Oh, what a tangled web we weave when first we practice to conceive.

DON HEROLD

You can sort of be married, you can sort of be divorced, you can sort of be living together, but you can't sort of have a baby.

DAVID SHIRE

When I found out I was pregnant, I was thrilled. It made me feel just like a high school girl again. Also, my condition really proved most eloquently the fact that I was loved—if only for a moment.

JOAN RIVERS

Pregnancy: Getting company inside one's skin.

MAGGIE SCARF

It's really a joyful time of your life, knowing you have this little life growing inside you moving all about. It's a miracle.

PHYLLIS ALSTON

There's no way to shorten pregnancy, not even by calendar reform.

STANISLAW J. LEC

I can feel the full weight of the body inside mine as it struggles to escape. It is heaving and throwing itself violently against my organs and my skin and my nerves.

ROSEANNE ARNOLD

Every woman should have a child. The sense of loss must be painful for those without a maternal relationship. There's nothing more warm and sensitive than a child. You complete the full range of emotions. For me, that's what living is all about.

DONNA KARAN

Journal for This Month

Second Month

Your breasts have begun to grow larger and sore. Morning sickness may have started, and, contrary to its name, morning sickness is not limited to the morning. It can happen any time—morning, noon, and night. You may also experience frequent urination, constipation, and dizziness and you may be more tired than usual. Any or none of these things may happen! Some foods you previously enjoyed may not appeal to you any longer.

The baby has grown to just about an inch by the end of the second month, with a human shape, and has arms and legs with the beginnings of fingers and toes. Its heart is beating and it has a brain. Tiny teeth buds are even growing in its jaws. All its main internal organs exist, although they are not fully developed.

11

We want better reasons for having children than not knowing how to prevent them.

DORA RUSSELL

Baby: Frequently can be classified as home accident.

MAX GRALNICK

We noticed that the bride was pregnant. So at the wedding everyone threw puffed rice.

DICK CAVETT

It knows nothing, and sleeps through all my agony, my sleeplessness, and the swirls of this swaying south wind.

AUVAIYAR

Have you ever met a woman who wasn't [anxious to have kids]? That's what they're built for. Their bodies tell them many times a month: children.

RICHARD GERE

In the creative process there is the father, the author of the play; the mother, the actor pregnant with the part; and the child, the role to be born.

KONSTANTIN SERGEEVICH ALEKSEEV STANISLAVSKI

I'll bet you one thing, if the man had to have the first baby there wouldn't be but two in the family. Yes sir, let him have the first one and the woman the next one, and his time wouldn't come around no more.

JOSEPHINE RILEY MATTHEWS

Motherhood is both a calling and an art and it demands of a woman…affection, gentleness, understanding…as well as firmness, restraint…and sacrifice.

SAMUEL L. BLUMENFELD

They caution pregnant women not to drink alcohol. It may harm the baby. I think that's ironic. If it wasn't for alcohol most women wouldn't be that way.

RITA RUDNER

The idea that birth can be both enjoyable and holy is immensely attractive.

MARINA HIRSCH

If one has plenty of money but no children, he cannot be reckoned rich: if one has children, but no money, he cannot be considered poor.

CHINESE PROVERB

Journal for This Month

Third Month

Morning sickness, if it was a problem, has probably disappeared by the end of the third month, though it sometimes lasts somewhat longer. With the enlargement of the uterus to about the size of an orange, your clothes are beginning to feel tight as your abdomen expands. Your breasts continue to enlarge. You may have food cravings and an increased appetite, although some foods previously enjoyed are no longer palatable.

At your complete medical examination which is usually given at this time, the doctor can probably hear the baby's heartbeat with a Doppler machine. The baby is about 3 inches long by the end of this month, and weighs about ½ ounce. Its muscles are developing, and the baby can open and close its mouth and fists.

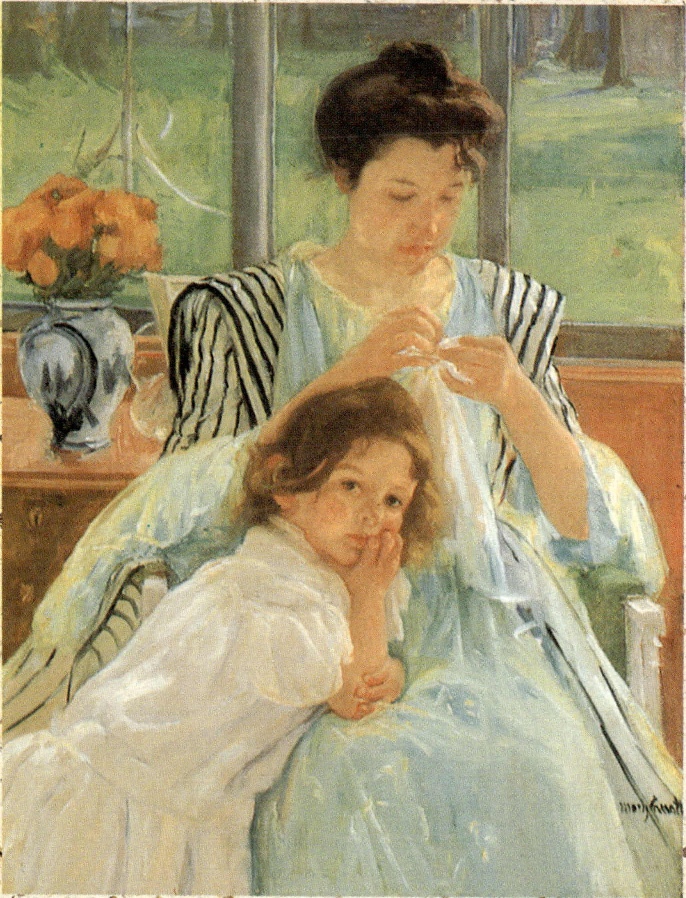

There's a depth linked to Sophie and the passion I have for her. I wouldn't have known about that without having had a child.

BETTE MIDLER

Great with child, and longing for stewed prunes.

SHAKESPEARE, *Measure for Measure*

When motherhood becomes the fruit of a deep yearning, not the result of ignorance or accident, its children will become the foundation of a new race.

MARGARET SANGER

Pregnancy agrees with me. I feel great.

DEMI MOORE

Pregnancy feels like a never ending process. The first six months go very quickly, but the last three months feel like they will never end.

PHYLLIS ALSTON

Journal for This Month

Fourth Month

$\mathcal{Y}$ou feel pretty good this month! You have more energy, less fatigue, and morning sickness has disappeared. Your appetite continues to be good, and maternity clothes are becoming the fashion of the day. Your nipples have gotten darker, and a dark line has appeared down the center of your abdomen. This may happen later in the pregnancy, or not at all.

The baby is completely formed, and is about 4 to 6 inches long. It weighs about 5 ounces and has swallowing and sucking reflexes.

21

The mother's heart is the child's schoolroom.

H. W. BEECHER

Pregnancy doesn't thrill me. Life is tough enough without someone kicking you from the inside.

RITA RUDNER

I wanted to feel it all. Feeling my body open up to allow a human being to pass through is the blessing, the gift. Having drugs would cheat me out of that.

DEMI MOORE

I think of Eve the first woman to give birth and how did she cope with this hideous pain that no one had ever before experienced.

ROSEANNE ARNOLD

If pregnancy were a book, they would cut the last two chapters.

NORA EPHRON

Journal for This Month

FIFTH MONTH

You feel more tired this month. Backaches and leg cramps may bother you. You may have nasal congestion and swelling of the hands and feet. Low heels are advisable from now on, and sleeping on your side may be more comfortable.

Usually between about the 19th and 22nd week, when the baby weighs about ½ pound, you may feel it moving around. Sometime around the 18th to 20th week your doctor can perform an ultrasound, and can see all the baby's organs and sometimes even identify the baby's sex.

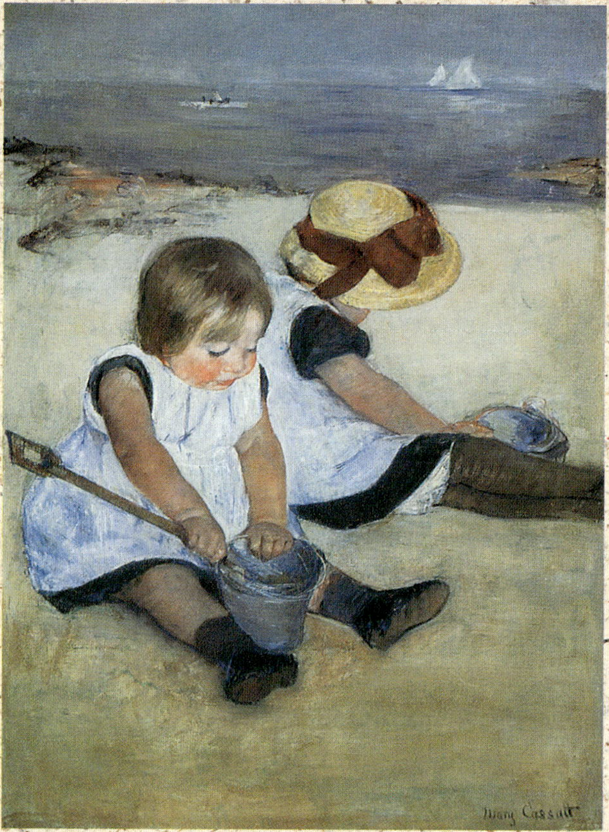
Mary Cassatt

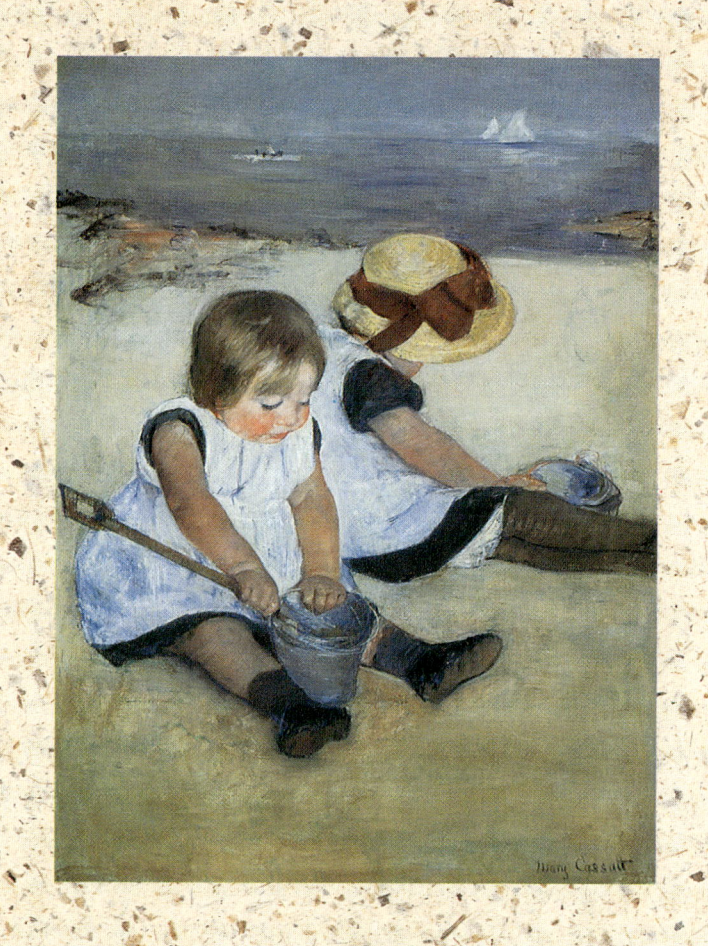

My wife—God bless her—was in labor for thirty-two hours. And I was faithful to her the entire time.

JONATHAN KATZ

When I was born, I was so surprised I couldn't talk for a year and a half.

GRACIE ALLEN

If women could remember pain, we would be a nation of single-child families.

BILL COSBY

He's a genius of a baby.

ANITA BAKER, ABOUT HER SON, WALTER

The pains of childbirth were altogether different from the enveloping effects of other kinds of pain. These were pains one could follow with one's mind.

MARGARET MEAD

Childbirth is more admirable than conquest, more amazing than self-defense, and as courageous as either one.

GLORIA STEINEM

When I was giving birth, the nurse asked, Still think blondes have more fun?

JOAN RIVERS

I stood in the hospital corridor the night after she was born. Through a window I could see all the small, crying newborn infants and somewhere among them slept the one who was mine. I stood there for hours filled with happiness until the night nurse sent me to bed.

LIV ULLMANN

Delivery is the wrong word to describe the childbearing process. *Delivery is: Here's your pizza. Takes thirty minutes or less. Exorcism,* I think, is more apt: *Please! Get the hell out of my body!*

JEFF STILSON

Giving birth is like trying to push a piano through a transom.

ALICE ROOSEVELT LONGWORTH

Journal for This Month

_____

_____

_____

_____

_____

_____

_____

_____

_____

_____

_____

_____

_____

_____

Sixth Month

Your uterus is expanding, and so is the skin on your abdomen, causing itching. Your growing tummy may cause your navel to pop out. Resting with your feet up is helpful when your feet swell. Heartburn is common.

By the end of this month the baby is about 10 to 13 inches long and weighs between 1 and 2 pounds. You can feel it kicking and moving around. The baby may suck its thumb, and buds for permanent teeth are forming. Loud sounds outside your body may startle the baby.

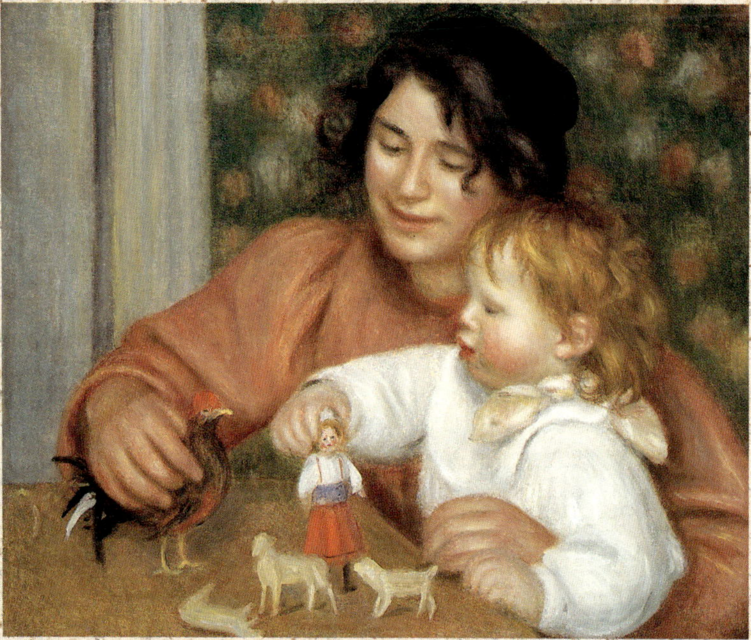

Childbirth of course is not the grand finale but one point, albeit a very dramatic one, in the process of becoming a mother.

SHEILA KITZINGER

I am… looking forward to the wonder-filled, miraculous moment when my husband and I greet our child for the first time. It is the most joyous time… there is no way to fully define or explain it.

IRENE BUBNACK

Death and taxes and childbirth! There's never any convenient time for any of them.

MARGARET MITCHELL

Mother didn't make it to the hospital. I was born on the bus. Mother was furious when she had to open her pocketbook the second time.

JACK DOUGLAS

The most wonderful sound our ears can hear is the sound of a new-born baby.

ANONYMOUS

The arrival of Julia was a personal, almost selfish pleasure, the kind that comes when another small person joins the cast of characters and enters the circle of those to care about, wonder about and watch.

ELLEN GOODMAN

Baby: A bald head and a pair of lungs.

EUGENE FIELD

The child was brought in, its infant beauty shining like a jewel in the greyness of the dawn.

MURASAKI SHIKIBU

$\mathscr{A}$ newborn baby is merely a small, noisy object, slightly fuzzy on one end, with no distinguishing marks to speak of except a mouth, and in color either a salmon pink or a deep sorrel, depending on whether it is going to grow up a blonde or a brunette. But to its immediate family it is without question the most phenomenal, the most astonishing, the most absolutely unparalleled thing that has yet occurred in the entire history of this planet.

IRVIN S. COBB

$\mathscr{H}$e's a very strong character, a tough little guy. He's very manly and has a swagger.

MEG RYAN, *ABOUT HER BABY, JACK HENRY*

Journal for This Month

SEVENTH MONTH

*A*s you gain weight this month, you may begin to have more physical complaints, like swelling, sleeping problems, more frequent heartburn, varicose veins. You may feel warm most of the time.

By the end of this month, the baby weighs about 3 pounds and responds to light, pain, and sound. In most cases the baby is capable of survival if born at the end of this period.

37

The thing about having a baby is that thereafter you have it.

JEAN KERR

You find out every woman, every pregnancy, every little baby's so unique. It was an experience I will never forget. A gift from God, that's the only thing you can say.

KATHIE LEE GIFFORD

Of all the joys that lighten suffering earth, what joy is welcomed like a new-born child?

CAROLINE NORTON

How beautifully everything is arranged by Nature; as soon as a child enters the world, it finds a mother ready to take care of it.

JULES MICHELET

I think a lot of women are intimidated by hospital nurses. I mean, here are all these women who have gone to school to learn all about babies! Even so, I've learned that if you see something being done with the baby you don't like, you shouldn't be afraid to tell the nurse. After all, it's YOUR baby!

JOAN LUNDEN

A baby really changes you. Everything I thought was so important before is really just silliness.

DEIDRE HALL

I couldn't wait to have children and continue the tradition. You need to watch your children at a very early age for aptitude in the fine arts, and you must have a plan for their development. You can't let your children decide everything they want to do.

DEBBIE ALLEN

𝒯he most important thing a mother can do to promote her child's future welfare is modeling a happy, fulfilled person—somebody who is taking care of her own needs, who's happy, who's playful, who's creative.

LOIS GOBRECHT

𝑀otherhood was a scary, unknown thing, and work was familiar and secure. Work gave me more esteem as a mom. I thought, Okay, I can handle my job. Surely I can handle being this precious little girl's mom.

LEEZA GIBBONS

𝒜 moment all new mothers know well: total exhaustion!

KATHIE LEE GIFFORD

Journal for This Month

Eighth Month

*D*iscomfort is more a fact of life for you now. Good posture can help you feel better. Breathlessness with exertion is common.

The baby is about 18 inches long and weighs about 5 pounds at the end of the eighth month. Its lungs may still be immature, but most other systems are well developed.

43

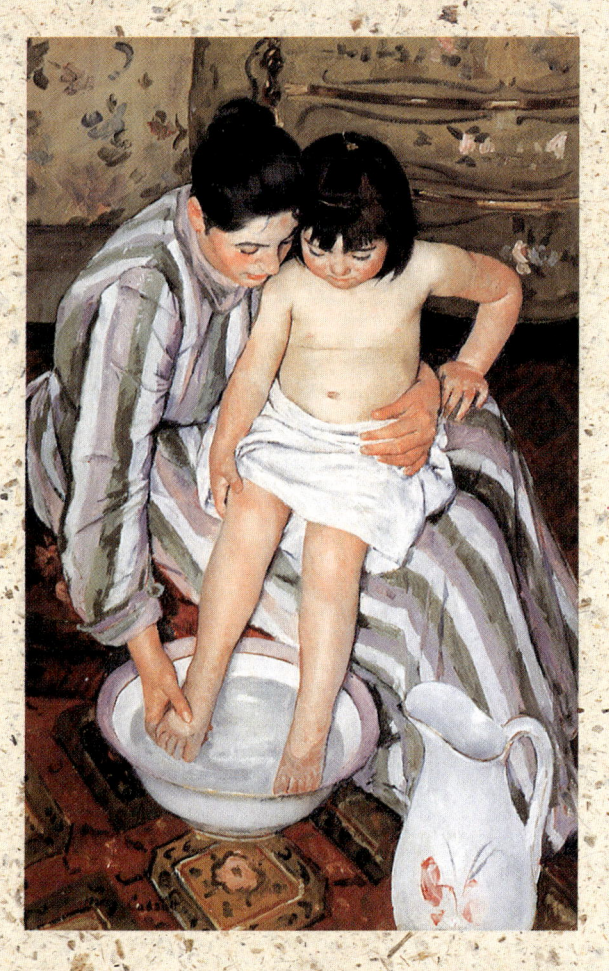

Who can foretell for what high cause this darling of the gods was born?

ANDREW MARVELL

The babe at first feeds upon the mother's bosom, but is always on her heart.

H. W. BEECHER

A baby is an angel whose wings decrease as his legs increase.

FRENCH PROVERB

We don't know how resourceful we are until we have a child. It is such a basic instinct to accommodate a child into one's life.

TINA BROWN

One of the most visible effects of a child's presence in the household is to turn the worthy parents into complete idiots when, without him, they would perhaps have remained mere imbeciles.

GEORGES COURTELINE

A child enters your home and makes so much noise for twenty years you can hardly stand it—then departs, leaving the house so silent you think you will go mad.

J. A. HOLMES

I knew having a baby would teach me about deep feelings of love, but I didn't know it would teach me so much about sharing.

DEIDRE HALL

Mothers of the race, the most important actors in the grand drama of human progress…

ELIZABETH CADY STANTON

A child learns self-control
    if she lives with praise.
She learns self-worth
    if she is given encouragement.
She learns right from wrong
    if she is treated fairly.
She learns to have a positive
    attitude if she feels secure.
She learns to find love in the
    world if she is surrounded by friends
    and family who love one another.

PHYLLIS ALSTON

Journal for This Month

_____

_____

_____

_____

_____

_____

_____

_____

_____

_____

_____

_____

_____

_____

Ninth Month

You're ready for this baby to be born now. In many cases it has dropped into position for birth, making breathing easier for you, and it is moving around less. You are seeing the doctor once a week, and your cervix is becoming ready for labor. Before you know it, the big day will be here!

The baby is getting ready for birth, too. Its lungs are mature now, and it has grown about 2 inches in length and 2½ pounds in weight. The average baby is about 7 pounds and 20 inches long at birth.

Finally you meet face to face, and heart to heart. Mother and baby are doing fine! Congratulations!

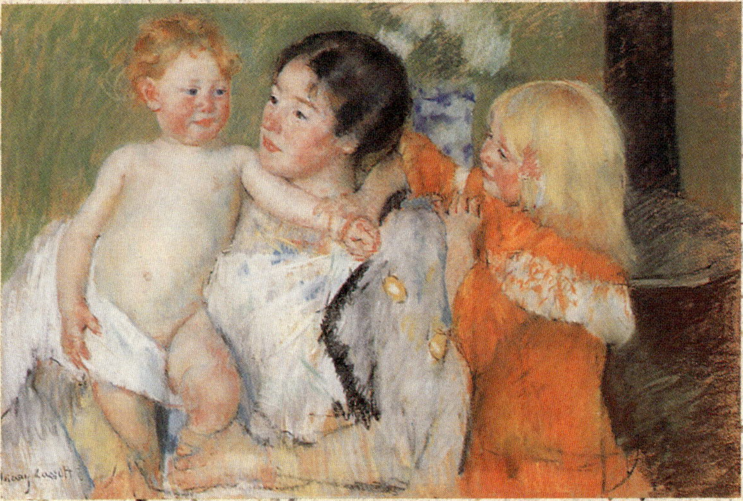

I think we're seeing in working mothers a change from *Thank God it's Friday* to *Thank God it's Monday*. If any working mother has not experienced that feeling, her children are not adolescent.

ANN DIEHL

I love these little people; and it is not a slight thing when they, who are so fresh from God, love us.

CHARLES DICKENS

*B*abies on television never spit up on the Ultrasuede.

ERMA BOMBECK

*T*he hand that rocks the cradle
Is the hand that rules the world.

WILLIAM ROSS WALLACE

*W*e find delight in the beauty and happiness of children that makes the heart too big for the body.

RALPH WALDO EMERSON

Journal for This Month

The First Year

*Y*ou're recovering from the birth of your child. The baby is growing every day, and it's hard to believe that you were carrying this infant inside you just a few weeks ago.

From the first month to the twelfth, the baby develops in various ways, but always bear in mind that babies develop at different rates.

At the same time, your life is changing in a multitude of ways. While this is one of the happiest times in a woman's life, many new mothers experience the blues, referred to as postpartum depression. This is common, but be assured it will pass. Don't neglect yourself. Get plenty of rest and avoid strenuous activity. After six weeks, visit your doctor for a postpartum checkup.

By now, you and your baby have gotten to

know each other. Together, you are settling into a routine. Questions you had six weeks ago that were overwhelming are now easily solved, and new questions are constantly arising to take their place. Never be reluctant to ask your obstetrician or pediatrician any question. You are not the first mother to feel uncertain, nor will you be the last. Remember, each child is unique. Their sleeping and feeding patterns vary greatly.

Before you know it, it's your baby's first birthday! You've overcome many hurdles—you've laughed, and you've cried, but it's certainly been one of the most exciting and rewarding journeys of your life.

Just imagine what the future holds!

DUE DATES

JAN.	1	2	3	4	5	6	7	8	9	10	11	12	13	14	15	16	17	18	19	20	21	22	23	24	25	26	27	28	29	30	31
OCT.	8	9	10	11	12	13	14	15	16	17	18	19	20	21	22	23	24	25	26	27	28	29	30	31	1	2	3	4	5	6	7
FEB.	1	2	3	4	5	6	7	8	9	10	11	12	13	14	15	16	17	18	19	20	21	22	23	24	25	26	27	28			
NOV.	8	9	10	11	12	13	14	15	16	17	18	19	20	21	22	23	24	25	26	27	28	29	30	1	2	3	4	5			
MAR.	1	2	3	4	5	6	7	8	9	10	11	12	13	14	15	16	17	18	19	20	21	22	23	24	25	26	27	28	29	30	31
DEC.	6	7	8	9	10	11	12	13	14	15	16	17	18	19	20	21	22	23	24	25	26	27	28	29	30	31	1	2	3	4	5
APRIL	1	2	3	4	5	6	7	8	9	10	11	12	13	14	15	16	17	18	19	20	21	22	23	24	25	26	27	28	29	30	
JAN.	6	7	8	9	10	11	12	13	14	15	16	17	18	19	20	21	22	23	24	25	26	27	28	29	30	31	1	2	3	4	
MAY	1	2	3	4	5	6	7	8	9	10	11	12	13	14	15	16	17	18	19	20	21	22	23	24	25	26	27	28	29	30	31
FEB.	5	6	7	8	9	10	11	12	13	14	15	16	17	18	19	20	21	22	23	24	25	26	27	28	1	2	3	4	5	6	7
JUNE	1	2	3	4	5	6	7	8	9	10	11	12	13	14	15	16	17	18	19	20	21	22	23	24	25	26	27	28	29	30	
MAR.	8	9	10	11	12	13	14	15	16	17	18	19	20	21	22	23	24	25	26	27	28	29	30	31	1	2	3	4	5	6	
JULY	1	2	3	4	5	6	7	8	9	10	11	12	13	14	15	16	17	18	19	20	21	22	23	24	25	26	27	28	29	30	31
APRIL	7	8	9	10	11	12	13	14	15	16	17	18	19	20	21	22	23	24	25	26	27	28	29	30	1	2	3	4	5	6	7
AUG.	1	2	3	4	5	6	7	8	9	10	11	12	13	14	15	16	17	18	19	20	21	22	23	24	25	26	27	28	29	30	31
MAY	8	9	10	11	12	13	14	15	16	17	18	19	20	21	22	23	24	25	26	27	28	29	30	31	1	2	3	4	5	6	7
SEPT.	1	2	3	4	5	6	7	8	9	10	11	12	13	14	15	16	17	18	19	20	21	22	23	24	25	26	27	28	29	30	
JUNE	8	9	10	11	12	13	14	15	16	17	18	19	20	21	22	23	24	25	26	27	28	29	30	1	2	3	4	5	6	7	
OCT.	1	2	3	4	5	6	7	8	9	10	11	12	13	14	15	16	17	18	19	20	21	22	23	24	25	26	27	28	29	30	31
JULY	8	9	10	11	12	13	14	15	16	17	18	19	20	21	22	23	24	25	26	27	28	29	30	31	1	2	3	4	5	6	7
NOV.	1	2	3	4	5	6	7	8	9	10	11	12	13	14	15	16	17	18	19	20	21	22	23	24	25	26	27	28	29	30	
AUG.	8	9	10	11	12	13	14	15	16	17	18	19	20	21	22	23	24	25	26	27	28	29	30	31	1	2	3	4	5	6	7
DEC.	1	2	3	4	5	6	7	8	9	10	11	12	13	14	15	16	17	18	19	20	21	22	23	24	25	26	27	28	29	30	31
SEPT.	7	8	9	10	11	12	13	14	15	16	17	18	19	20	21	22	23	24	25	26	27	28	29	30	1	2	3	4	5	6	7

Look for the date of the first day of your last menstrual period in the bold print above the horizontal line. The date below it is your baby's estimated time of arrival.

$\mathcal{I}$ think of birth as the search for a larger apartment.

RITA MAE BROWN

$\mathcal{F}$inally, simply, if I hadn't had a child, I'd never have known that most elemental, direct, true relationship. I don't know if I'd fully understand the values of society that I prize. I would have missed some of the mystery of life and death. Not to know how a child grows, the wonder of a newborn's hand…. I have been fortunate.

DIANNE FEINSTEIN

$\mathcal{T}$here are only two lasting bequests we can give our children—one is roots, the other wings.

ANONYMOUS

$\mathcal{A}$ baby is God's opinion that the world should go on.

CARL SANDBURG

Acknowledgments

Page 5. Mary Cassatt, *Reine Lefebvre Holding a Nude Baby*, (1902). Oil on canvas. Worcester Art Museum, Worcester, Massachusetts.

Page 11. Mary Cassatt, *Hélène de Septeuil*, (1889). Pastel on beige paper. The William Benton Museum of Art, The University of Connecticut. Louise Crombie Beach Memorial Collection.

Page 17. Mary Cassatt, *Young Mother Sewing*, (ca. 1900). Oil on canvas. The Metropolitan Museum of Art, Bequest of Mrs. H. O. Havemeyer, 1929. The H. O. Havemeyer Collection. (29.100.48)

Page 21. Mary Cassatt, *Mother and Child*, (1889). Oil on canvas. The Roland P. Murdock Collection, Wichita Art Museum, Wichita, Kansas.

Page 25. Mary Cassatt, *Children Playing on the Beach*, (1884). Oil on canvas. Ailsa Mellon Bruce Collection, © 1993 National Gallery of Art, Washington, D.C.

Page 31. Auguste Renoir, *Child with Toys - Gabrielle and the Artist's Son, Jean*, (ca. 1894), Oil on canvas. Collection of Mr. and Mrs. Paul Mellon, © 1993 National Gallery of Art, Washington, D.C.

Page 37. Mary Cassatt, *Women Admiring a Child*, (1897). Pastel on paper. © The Detroit Institute of Arts, Gift of Edward Chandler Walker.

Page 43. Mary Cassatt, American, 1844-1926, *The Bath*, Oil on canvas, 1891/92, 39-1/2 x 26 in., Robert A. Waller Fund, 1910.2. Photograph © 1993 The Art Institute of Chicago. All Rights Reserved.

Page 49. *After the Bath*. Pastel, ca. 1901, 64.8 x 99.7 cm. Mary Cassatt, American, 1845-1926. © The Cleveland Museum of Art, Gift of J. H. Wade, 20.379.